EDGE BOOKS

X-SPORTS

KITEBOARDING

BY ERIC PRESZLER

CONSULTANT:
MARK BEGLE
SKYHIGH KITEBOARDING
MARTHA'S VINEYARD, MASSACHUSETTS

Capstone press

Mankato, Minnesota

Edge Books are published by Capstone Press,
151 Good Counsel Drive, P.O. Box 669, Mankato, Minnesota 56002.
www.capstonepress.com

Library of Congress Cataloging-in-Publication Data
Preszler, Eric.
    Kiteboarding / by Eric Preszler.
    p. cm.—(Edge books. X-sports)
    Includes bibliographical references and index.
    ISBN 0-7368-3783-3 (hardcover)
    1. Kite surfing—Juvenile literature. I. Title. II. Series.
GV840.K49P74 2005
796.1'5—dc22   2004021611

J796.1
PRE

Summary: Discusses the sport of kiteboarding, including gear needed, tricks, and
    famous kiteboarders.

Editorial Credits
Connie Colwell Miller, editor; Jason Knudson, set designer; Enoch Peterson and
    Linda Clavel, book designers; Jason D. Miller, illustrator; Jo Miller,
    photo researcher; Scott Thoms, photo editor

Photo Credits
AP/Wide World Photos/Jason Arthurs, 14 (bottom)
Corbis/Mark A. Johnson, 10, 13; NewSport/Jonathan Selkowitz, 11, 20, 23 (bottom);
    Rick Doyle, 6; Reuters/Kimberly White, 9
Digital Vision, 7
Ethan Janson, 21
Getty Images Inc./Mark Dadswell, 18; Ryan McVay, cover, 5, 17
Red Bull/Clay Rogers, 23 (top), 27; Dean Treml, 29
Zuma/Palm Beach Post/Greg Lovett, 14 (top)

1 2 3 4 5 6 10 09 08 07 06 05

TABLE OF CONTENTS

CHAPTER 1

KITEBOARDING

A breeze blows across the beach, and the sun shines. The weather is perfect for kiteboarding. A large colorful kite flies in the blue sky. A woman riding a board in the water controls the kite. Soon, the kite catches a strong gust of wind.

The kite lifts the kiteboarder high above the water. People on the beach wonder if she'll ever land. After reaching a height of nearly 40 feet (12 meters), the kiteboarder drifts back down. She lands gently on the water 80 feet (24 meters) from where she set sail.

LEARN ABOUT:

- The Legaignoux brothers
- Inflatable frames
- Kiteboarding today

Large, colorful kites pull kiteboarders as they ride their boards.

KITEBOARDING HISTORY

Kiteboarding can actually be done on land, water, or snow. Kiteboarding is a combination of kite flying, wakeboarding, windsurfing, surfing, and snowboarding. Kiteboarding is one of the fastest growing extreme sports.

Bruno and Dominique Legaignoux built the first kiteboarding kite. In 1984, these French brothers built a kite with an inflatable frame.

EDGE FACT

The Legaignoux brothers first used water skis to try out kites.

This structure was filled with air to create the kite's shape. The inflatable frame allowed the kite to float on the water so kiteboarders could relaunch it when it crashed. The Legaignoux brothers continued to improve their kite designs for the next 20 years.

By the late 1990s, kiteboarding increased in popularity. In 1998, 250 people bought kites. By 2001, 50,000 people bought kites from 20 companies.

Kiteboarding shares some features with the sport of windsurfing.

CHAPTER 2

KITEBOARDING GEAR

Kiteboarders need more than just water and wind to fly in the sky. They need a kite, a board, and safety gear. Kiteboarders wear wet suits to stay warm in cold weather. They wear board shorts in warm weather.

KITES

Kiteboarding kites are made of lightweight material similar to a parachute. Most kites have inflatable frames. The frame keeps the kite afloat in water. The kite and the frame together only weigh about 2 pounds (.9 kilogram).

LEARN ABOUT:

- Types of kites
- Control bar
- Staying safe

Kiteboarding kites have inflatable frames.

Different shapes of kites pull kiteboarders at different speeds.

Kiteboarders can choose between low aspect kites or high aspect kites. A low aspect kite is best for beginners. This type of kite is wide. The width of the kite helps it relaunch easier. Low aspect kites pull kiteboarders at a slow and steady pace.

More advanced kiteboarders use a high aspect kite. This kite is narrow. The shape of this kite allows it to travel more quickly. It also produces more lift for jumping. High aspect kites are difficult to relaunch when crashed.

BOARDS

Kiteboards are constantly changing. Kiteboarders can choose from different shapes of boards to suit their needs. Wakeboard style boards are the most popular. They have foot straps to help keep the kiteboarder attached to the board while in the air.

Kiteboarding boards look like surfboards with foot straps.

HARNESSES AND CONTROL BAR

All kiteboarders use a harness to connect to the kite. Kiteboarders wear a harness around their waists. When the kite flies in the air, the harness pulls on the kiteboarder's body instead of on the arms. This keeps the kiteboarder from getting too tired.

Kiteboarders direct the movement of the kite with the control bar. The control bar is connected to the kite by the flying lines. Kites are controlled by two or four flying lines. Pulling left or right steers the kite. Pushing the control bar up or down controls the power of the kite.

EDGE FACT

Tea-bagging is when the wind lifts and then dunks a kiteboarder in the water more than once.

A harness around the waist prevents injury to the kiteboarder's shoulders and elbows.

Kiteboarders direct the movement of their kites with a control bar.

Proper safety gear helps prevent injuries.

SAFETY

Kiteboarders must learn to control their kites before they go out on the water. Kites are powerful when they are soaring in the air. Kites have safety systems to help prevent injury.

The safety leash connects the control bar to the kiteboarder's wrist. If the rider lets go of the control bar, the leash pulls a line connected to the kite. The kite instantly folds up and stops pulling the kiteboarder.

Training is one of the most important safety measures for kiteboarders. Kiteboarders attend Professional Air Sports Association (PASA) schools to learn kiteboarding skills. These schools teach proper equipment use and safety skills. Kiteboarding is an exciting sport and must be practiced safely.

Kiteboarders need to be more than just good swimmers. They need a great deal of practice controlling their kites on land before they go into the water.

CHAPTER 3

KITEBOARDING TRICKS

Kiteboarding is a challenging sport. Keeping the kite soaring while balancing on a board is difficult enough. But many kiteboarders can perform tricks while kiteboarding.

BASIC SKILLS

Kiteboarders first learn to jump, or boost. To jump, kiteboarders fly their kites in a way to produce lift. They pull the control bar close to their body and quickly lift their lead hand. This move changes the angle of the kite so it catches more air. Kiteboarders turn the board against the kite. The kite then pulls them into the air.

LEARN ABOUT:

- **The jump**
- **The airpass**
- **Red Bull King of the Air**

Keeping a kite soaring while balancing on a board is a challenging task.

Kiteboarders need to master basic skills like jumping before they begin to learn tricks.

Kiteboarders also must learn to land safely. To land, kiteboarders position the kite over their head. As the kite begins to descend, the kiteboarders turn the board away from the wind. Next, the kiteboarders extend their legs. When the board lands, kiteboarders squat to absorb the impact.

INTERMEDIATE TRICKS

Kiteboarders perform many of the same tricks that skateboarders or snowboarders do. Kiteboarders do a nose grab. To do a nose grab, they hold the nose of the board with one hand while soaring in the air. Kiteboarders can also perform an indy air. While in the air, they grab the toe edge of the board between their feet.

The challenge of these grabs is to hold on to the control bar. Kiteboarders cannot drop their control bar during their moves. They will lose control of their kites if they do.

Kiteboarders must hold on to the control bar at all times or they will lose control of their kites.

Advanced tricks include doing a flip.

ADVANCED TRICKS

One of the most challenging kiteboarding tricks is the airpass. This trick is a backflip with a 180-degree or 360-degree spin. Kiteboarders perform an airpass by pulling on the control bar and flipping upside down in the air. While upside down, they twist their bodies to hold the bar behind them. Next, they lower their feet and rotate the board right before landing in the water.

The most advanced kiteboarders perform tricks in competitions like the Red Bull King of the Air contest. Combining advanced tricks, such as spins, flips, and grabs, into one super trick impresses the judges at this contest. Red Bull King of the Air is held in Maui, Hawaii. People consider the Red Bull King of the Air contest the most important kiteboarding event today. Kiteboarders can win a prize of $20,000 at this contest.

EDGE FACT

Kiteboarders say that a kite has "grunt" when a kite has a great deal of power.

Kiteboarders perform advanced tricks in competitions.

Kiteboarders remove their feet from their foot straps during some tricks.

HOW TO DO A GRAB

1. While soaring in the air, the kiteboarder lets go of the control bar with one hand.

2. The kiteboarder reaches a hand toward the edge of the board.

3. The kiteboarder grabs the board with one hand and controls the kite with the other.

4. The kiteboarder lets go of the board and straightens both legs.

CHAPTER 4

FAMOUS KITEBOARDERS

Kiteboarding is still a new sport. Some of the most successful kiteboarders today are working to increase the sport's popularity.

JULIE GILBERT

Julie Gilbert was a windsurfer. In 1998, she visited Maui to windsurf the waves. In Maui, she met her future husband. He introduced her to kiteboarding.

Seven months later, Gilbert took second place in her first kiteboarding event. The event was the Red Bull King of the Air contest.

LEARN ABOUT:

- Julie Gilbert
- "Flash" Austin
- Charles Deleau

Julie Gilbert holds the women's world record for hang time in kiteboarding.

In 2001, Gilbert won the World Championship in the freestyle and hang time competitions. She set a world record for hang time at this event. She then went on to break her own record at the 2002 Red Bull King of the Air contest. She hung in the air on her kiteboard for 6.48 seconds.

"FLASH" AUSTIN

Marcus "Flash" Austin is one of kiteboarding's best-known athletes. Austin's flashy tricks increased the popularity of pro kiteboarding. Austin won the World Championship of Kiteboarding in 2000. He was also the first person to kiteboard across the 70-mile (113-kilometer) stretch of water from Norway to Denmark.

In the late 1990s, Austin and about 35 other kiteboarders created their own beach for kiteboarding. Ka'a Point in Hawaii was littered with trash and rocks. Austin and his friends cleaned up the beach and began to kiteboard there. Today, Ka'a Point is known as Kite Beach.

CHARLES DELEAU

Many kiteboarders grew up near sunny beaches and oceansides. Charles Deleau spent much of his youth near a lake in northeastern France. Deleau didn't start kiteboarding until 2000.

Deleau enjoyed kiteboarding as soon as he tried it. In 2003, he placed first in the Kiteboarding World Cup. He won the Red Bull King of the Air contest in December 2003.

Kiteboarding continues to grow. Future stars may just be learning the sport today.

"Flash" Austin has helped make pro kiteboarding more popular.

GLOSSARY

airpass (AIR-pass)—a kiteboarding trick that involves a backflip and a spin

control bar (kuhn-TROHL BAR)—a bar that kiteboarders use to control the movement of their kite

descend (dee-SEND)—to move from a higher place to a lower place

grab (GRAB)—a move in which kiteboarders grab part of the board with one hand

harness (HAR-niss)—a device that straps one thing to another

inflatable (in-FLAY-tuh-buhl)–something that can be filled with air and expanded; kiteboarding kites have inflatable frames.

lead hand (LEED HAND)—the hand that is closest to the front of the board in the direction that the boarder is traveling

READ MORE

Voeller, Edward A. *Extreme Surfing.* Extreme Sports. Mankato, Minn.: Capstone Press, 2000.

Woods, Bob. *Water Sports.* Extreme Sports. Milwaukee: Gareth Stevens, 2004.

INTERNET SITES

FactHound offers a safe, fun way to find Internet sites related to this book. All of the sites on FactHound have been researched by our staff.

Here's how:

1. Visit *www.facthound.com*
2. Type in this special code **0736837833** for age-appropriate sites. Or enter a search word related to this book for a more general search.
3. Click on the **Fetch It** button.

FactHound will fetch the best sites for you!

INDEX